THE EVIDENCE BEHIND DONALD TRUMP'S IMPEACHMENT

And the Real Reason Democrats Want Him Removed From Office

Maxwell Lane

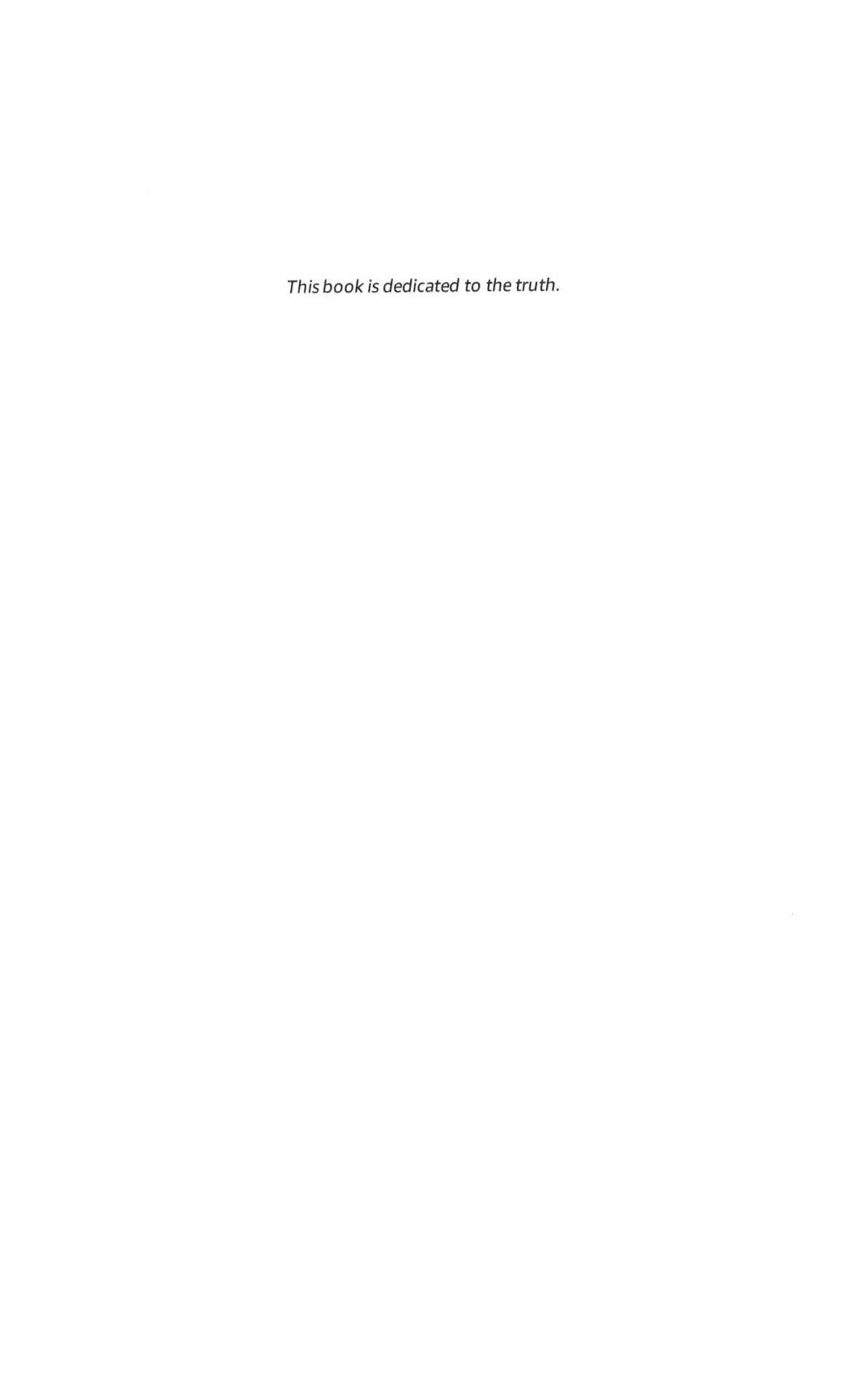

This book is dedicated to the truth.

MAXWELL LANE

Author's Note

All information included in this book is factual and certified as being 100% accurate. Countless hours were dedicated to discovering the answer to one of America's greatest topics of debate. I encourage you to do your own independent research in order to validate all information presented.

CHAPTER 1

They lost 2016 and can't win 2020.

CHAPTER 2

They lost 2016 and can't win 2020.

CHAPTER 3

They lost 2016 and can't win 2020.

CHAPTER 4

They lost 2016 and can't win 2020.

CHAPTER 5

They lost 2016 and can't win 2020.

CHAPTER 6

They lost 2016 and can't win 2020.

CHAPTER 7

They lost 2016 and can't win 2020.

CHAPTER 8

They lost 2016 and can't win 2020.

◆ ◆ ◆

CHAPTER 9

They lost 2016 and can't win 2020.

❖ ❖ ❖

CHAPTER 10

They lost 2016 and can't win 2020.

CHAPTER 11

They lost 2016 and can't win 2020.

CHAPTER 12

They lost 2016 and can't win 2020.

CHAPTER 13

They lost 2016 and can't win 2020.

◆ ◆ ◆

CHAPTER 14

They lost 2016 and can't win 2020.

CHAPTER 15

They lost 2016 and can't win 2020.

◆ ◆ ◆

CHAPTER 16

They lost 2016 and can't win 2020.

❖ ❖ ❖

CHAPTER 17

They lost 2016 and can't win 2020.

CHAPTER 18

They lost 2016 and can't win 2020.

CHAPTER 19

They lost 2016 and can't win 2020.

CHAPTER 20

They lost 2016 and can't win 2020.

CHAPTER 21

They lost 2016 and can't win 2020.

CHAPTER 22

They lost 2016 and can't win 2020.

CHAPTER 23

They lost 2016 and can't win 2020.

CHAPTER 24

They lost 2016 and can't win 2020.

❖ ❖ ❖

CHAPTER 25

They lost 2016 and can't win 2020.

◆ ◆ ◆

CHAPTER 26

They lost 2016 and can't win 2020.

CHAPTER 27

They lost 2016 and can't win 2020.

CHAPTER 28

They lost 2016 and can't win 2020.

CHAPTER 29

They lost 2016 and can't win 2020.

◆ ◆ ◆

CHAPTER 30

They lost 2016 and can't win 2020.

CHAPTER 31

They lost 2016 and can't win 2020.

◆ ◆ ◆

CHAPTER 32

They lost 2016 and can't win 2020.

CHAPTER 33

They lost 2016 and can't win 2020.

CHAPTER 34

They lost 2016 and can't win 2020.

◆ ◆ ◆

CHAPTER 35

They lost 2016 and can't win 2020.

CHAPTER 36

They lost 2016 and can't win 2020.

❖ ❖ ❖

CHAPTER 37

They lost 2016 and can't win 2020.

CHAPTER 38

They lost 2016 and can't win 2020.

CHAPTER 39

They lost 2016 and can't win 2020.

CHAPTER 40

They lost 2016 and can't win 2020.

CHAPTER 41

They lost 2016 and can't win 2020.

❖ ❖ ❖

CHAPTER 42

They lost 2016 and can't win 2020.

CHAPTER 43

They lost 2016 and can't win 2020.

CHAPTER 44

They lost 2016 and can't win 2020.

◆ ◆ ◆

CHAPTER 45

Donald Trump is draining the swamp.

www.ingramcontent.com/pod-product-compliance
Lightning Source LLC
Chambersburg PA
CBHW020600220526
45463CB00006B/2383